Samuel Adams

Patriot

Colonial Leaders

Lord Baltimore
English Politician and Colonist

Benjamin Banneker
American Mathematician and Astronomer

Sir William Berkeley
Governor of Virginia

William Bradford
Governor of Plymouth Colony

Jonathan Edwards
Colonial Religious Leader

Benjamin Franklin
American Statesman, Scientist, and Writer

Anne Hutchinson
Religious Leader

Cotton Mather
Author, Clergyman, and Scholar

Increase Mather
Clergyman and Scholar

James Oglethorpe
Humanitarian and Soldier

William Penn
Founder of Democracy

Sir Walter Raleigh
English Explorer and Author

Caesar Rodney
American Patriot

John Smith
English Explorer and Colonist

Miles Standish
Plymouth Colony Leader

Peter Stuyvesant
Dutch Military Leader

George Whitefield
Clergyman and Scholar

Roger Williams
Founder of Rhode Island

John Winthrop
Politician and Statesman

John Peter Zenger
Free Press Advocate

Revolutionary War Leaders

John Adams
Second U.S. President

Samuel Adams
Patriot

Ethan Allen
Revolutionary Hero

Benedict Arnold
Traitor to the Cause

John Burgoyne
British General

George Rogers Clark
American General

Lord Cornwallis
British General

Thomas Gage
British General

King George III
English Monarch

Nathanael Greene
Military Leader

Nathan Hale
Revolutionary Hero

Alexander Hamilton
First U.S. Secretary of the Treasury

John Hancock
President of the Continental Congress

Patrick Henry
American Statesman and Speaker

William Howe
British General

John Jay
First Chief Justice of the Supreme Court

Thomas Jefferson
Author of the Declaration of Independence

John Paul Jones
Father of the U.S. Navy

Thaddeus Kosciuszko
Polish General and Patriot

Lafayette
French Freedom Fighter

James Madison
Father of the Constitution

Francis Marion
The Swamp Fox

James Monroe
American Statesman

Thomas Paine
Political Writer

Molly Pitcher
Heroine

Paul Revere
American Patriot

Betsy Ross
American Patriot

Baron Von Steuben
American General

George Washington
First U.S. President

Anthony Wayne
American General

Famous Figures of the Civil War Era

John Brown
Abolitionist

Jefferson Davis
Confederate President

Frederick Douglass
Abolitionist and Author

Stephen A. Douglas
Champion of the Union

David Farragut
Union Admiral

Ulysses S. Grant
Military Leader and President

Stonewall Jackson
Confederate General

Joseph E. Johnston
Confederate General

Robert E. Lee
Confederate General

Abraham Lincoln
Civil War President

George Gordon Meade
Union General

George McClellan
Union General

William Henry Seward
Senator and Statesman

Philip Sheridan
Union General

William Sherman
Union General

Edwin Stanton
Secretary of War

Harriet Beecher Stowe
Author of Uncle Tom's Cabin

James Ewell Brown Stuart
Confederate General

Sojourner Truth
Abolitionist, Suffragist, and Preacher

Harriet Tubman
Leader of the Underground Railroad

Revolutionary War Leaders

Samuel Adams

Patriot

Veda Boyd Jones

Arthur M. Schlesinger, jr.
Senior Consulting Editor

Chelsea House Publishers

Philadelphia

CHELSEA HOUSE PUBLISHERS
Editor-in-Chief Sally Cheney
Director of Production Kim Shinners
Production Manager Pamela Loos
Art Director Sara Davis
Production Editor Diann Grasse

Staff for *SAMUEL ADAMS*
Editor Sally Cheney
Associate Art Director Takeshi Takahashi
Series Design Keith Trego
Cover Design 21st Century Publishing and Communications, Inc.
Picture Researcher Jane Sanders
Layout 21st Century Publishing and Communications, Inc.

The Chelsea House World Wide Web address is
http://www.chelseahouse.com

First Printing
1 3 5 7 9 8 6 4 2

Library of Congress Cataloging-in-Publication Data

Jones, Veda Boyd.
   Samuel Adams / Veda Boyd Jones.
      p. cm. — (Revolutionary War leaders)
   Includes bibliographical references and index.
   ISBN 0-7910-6368-0 (hc : alk. paper) — ISBN 0-7910-6387-9
(pbk. : alk. paper)
   1. Adams, Samuels, 1722-1803—Juvenile literature. 2. Politicians
—United States-Biography—Juvenile literature. 3. United States.
Declaration of Independence—Signers—Biography—Juvenile
literature. 4. United States—History—Revolution, 1775-1783—
Biography—Juvenile literature. [1. Adams, Samuel, 1722-1803.
2. Politicians. 3. United States—History—Revolution, 1775-1783.]
I. Title. II. Series.

E302.6.A2 J66 2001
977.3'13'092—dc21
  [B]   2001028528

Publisher's Note: In Colonial and Revolutionary War America, there were no standard rules for spelling, punctuation, capitalization, or grammar. Some of the quotations that appear in the Colonial Leaders and Revolutionary War Leaders series come from original documents and letters written during this time in history. Original quotations reflect writing inconsistencies of the period.

Contents

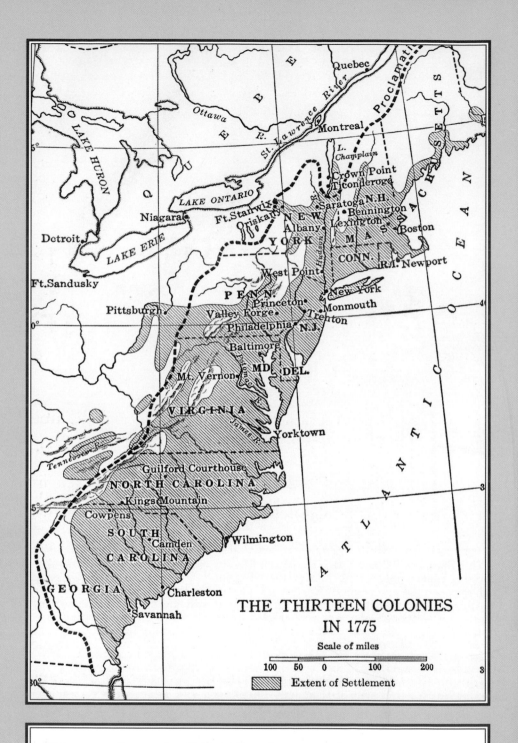

THE THIRTEEN COLONIES
IN 1775

Scale of miles

100 50 0 100 200

Extent of Settlement

This map shows the 13 British colonies in America in 1775.

Growing Up in Boston

S amuel Adams was born at noon on September 27, 1722, in Boston, the biggest town in the Massachusetts **colony**. He was named after his father, who was called Deacon Samuel Adams, because he was an assistant in the Congregational Church. His mother, Mary, hoped that Samuel would grow up to be a minister.

Massachusetts was not a state at the time Samuel was born, because the United States had not been formed yet. Great Britain, a country far across the Atlantic Ocean, controlled the colony. Britain was ruled by a king, who also ruled the conoly.

Samuel's father owned a brewery on Purchase Street, and the family lived in a large house next door. Deacon Adams was a good businessman and a town leader. During his life he held several political offices and was elected to the Massachusetts House of Representatives.

Deacon Adams started the Caucus Club in Boston. Its members were working-class people. They were shipyard workers, craftsmen, carpenters, and shopkeepers. The club met and talked about politics. Members decided who should be elected to important positions. Then they tried to talk people into voting for their candidates. They wanted men who would tell the British governor of the colony what he could do to be elected.

As a young boy, Samuel listened to members of the Caucus Club as they discussed politics. If they disagreed with the British governor, they would decide how to rile the colonists to take action.

Samuel's education started in church. Like the rest of his family, he spent about four hours on Sunday listening to the preacher, singing songs, and praying. Samuel's favorite part was singing. He was a very smart boy. By the age of three, he had memorized the Lord's Prayer.

Like other young boys and girls, Samuel attended a **dame school**. He was taught reading, writing, and arithmetic. When he was seven, Samuel began his studies at the Boston Latin School. There Samuel was taught that learning was more important than money.

Samuel graduated from the school in the spring of 1736. At the graduation ceremony, he made a speech in Latin. In the fall he crossed the Charles River to attend college at Harvard. He was only 14 years old when he moved away from home, which was common at that time.

In the dormitory, several boys lived in a large room with Samuel. They got up at five each morning, and at six the bell rang for morning prayers. Breakfast was bread and ale, followed by classes at eight. Lunch was more bread and ale. Studies and activities continued until five, when it was time for more prayers. Dinner was at seven-thirty, and this time Samuel and the other boys received meat with their bread. At nine the boys went to bed. Saturday was spent studying religion. Sunday was a day filled with church activities.

Samuel studied Hebrew, Latin, Greek, philosophy, science, writing, and speaking. He was especially good at writing. He studied many political essays to see how they were written. The ideas of John Locke, a 17th century Englishman, interested him. Locke wrote that all men should be politically equal and have three basic rights—to life, liberty, and property. He believed government did not have the right to tax people without the consent of the people through their elected representatives. Locke also believed that people should resist bad government and overthrow **tyrants**.

Samuel copied Locke's ideas in his notebook and read them over and over. Locke's thinking fell in line with the thinking of the Caucus

Club. Samuel took these ideas as his own.

About this same time, Samuel heard Reverend George Whitefield preach. He said religious people should return to the Puritan ways of their forefathers. Simple dress, hard work, and strong faith were demanded of God-fearing people. Samuel agreed with these religious ideas. He thought the love of money led to selfishness and turned people away from God.

He didn't have to change much about himself to fit with his religious beliefs. He didn't care about his appearance. When his parents sent him a new suit, he wouldn't wear it because he thought the old suit was good enough. He didn't like the fad of wearing wigs and wore his own hair uncovered. He didn't care for gambling at cards, horseracing, or ball games. Even though he adopted simple religious ways, he decided not to become a minister. He wanted to learn about government.

At age 17, Samuel graduated from Harvard.

Samuel left home to attend Harvard College in Cambridge, Massachusetts, in the fall of 1736.

He decided to continue at Harvard's graduate school and earn a master's degree. Samuel followed in his father's footsteps and made friends with the working-class people of Boston. He was generous, and many times he gave money to a friend in need. He loved sitting in a tavern with friends and talking about government.

The poorer people knew that Samuel was different from other Harvard men. Money, fame, and power were of no interest to Samuel. He listened to another man's opinion before he gave his own. And he listened carefully and looked the man in the eye while he was speaking. Then he tried to talk the man into agreeing with his own opinion. Samuel's own opinion always dealt with the right to liberty.

While Samuel was deep into studies, his family faced financial ruin. Deacon Adams and a few of his friends had started a Land Bank. This bank lent money to small businesses and farmers. The wealthy

If a crowd of 12 or more threatened the peace, a British official could read the Riot Act. If the group did not break up within one hour, members could be arrested and jailed. The fine for this crime could be as harsh as life in prison. The official had to read the entire act, including the words "God save the King." Of course if the mob was unruly, many rioters could claim they couldn't hear all the words and have the charges dismissed.

people in town didn't like the bank. They convinced the **British Parliament** to declare the bank illegal. Deacon Adams's bank went out of business, and he and his friends owed large amounts of money. Samuel's father lost a large part of his fortune.

British officials in Massachusetts wanted Deacon Adams to sell his house and brewery to pay off the debt. Samuel's father refused to sell, and many colonists sided with him. Samuel wanted to leave school and get a job to help out. But his father wouldn't allow it. Instead, to save money Samuel left the boardinghouse where he lived and moved back to the Harvard campus. He waited tables in the dining room to earn free meals.

Samuel was angry with wealthy lawmaker Thomas Hutchinson and other colonists who sided with the British on the Land Bank issue. Samuel thought the British had violated the rights of a man to own his own property.

In 1743, Samuel finished his master's degree

at Harvard. At the graduation ceremony, he spoke in Latin about resisting a bad government if the welfare of the people was at stake. He stated John Locke's ideas of rebelling against a tyrant, but he didn't mention Britain's rule or the king. If he had mentioned them, he would be guilty of treason and might even be hanged.

Samuel was not careful with his money. He was only interested in politics.

2

A Failure in Business

Samuel needed a job. Since his passion was politics, he thought he should be a lawyer. To learn about the law, he worked for a lawyer. But he didn't want to sue people. He wanted to work for human rights. His mother convinced him that lawyers were more interested in money than in justice. He stopped studying law.

Next he worked as a clerk in a counting house. This was like working in a bank. Samuel made entries in big ledger books and added and subtracted amounts of money.

The best thing about this job was the noon hour.

Samuel was allowed one hour to eat the mid-day meal. He went to taverns and talked to other diners about politics. Samuel wanted the people to have more power in government. He wanted the British Parliament to have less power. Many times the talks were so interesting, he didn't make it back to work on time. He left this job after a few months.

Deacon Adams gave Samuel 1,000 British pounds to start a business. It could be any business. But Samuel didn't know what kind of business to start. His only interest was politics, but that wasn't a business.

The money disappeared quickly. Samuel lent half of it to a friend, who could not repay it. The other half he spent here and there. He could not manage his money while he was busy thinking about politics.

His father hired him at the brewery. Samuel was paid, but he probably didn't do any work. Instead he spoke to people about their rights.

Samuel and some friends started the Whipping-Post Club. The name stood for the way the members talked against British officials. Samuel was in charge of their short-lived newspaper, the *Public Advertiser*. He wrote most of it, and his articles were about liberty and the people's rights to have a voice in government.

In early 1748, Samuel's father died. A year later, his mother died. Samuel was 26 and had inherited the brewery business and the house on Purchase Street.

Samuel had been seeing the preacher's daughter, Elizabeth Checkley. They were married on October 17, 1749, and lived in the Adams's family home.

Even though he was owner of the brewery, the business did not interest Samuel. In 1756, he was elected as a tax collector. For a man who didn't have much skill with money, this was a bad choice. If a person owed taxes, but couldn't pay, Samuel understood. He didn't collect many taxes, which was not good. As tax collector, he was to pay for those who didn't pay. And he didn't have much money. The brewery was going into a lot of debt.

While Samuel worked at these two jobs, Elizabeth kept the household running. In all, she had six children, but three died as babies. A few weeks after having her sixth baby, who was born dead, Elizabeth died. That left Samuel to take care of five-year-old Samuel and one-year-old Hannah.

Samuel was an odd sight as he walked the streets of Boston in his worn red cloak, his only coat. He wore no wig, like others around him. His hands shook and his head nodded from a disease that caused tremors, or shaking.

He talked with everyone he met about liberty and the rights of the people.

Samuel Adams suffered from what is believed to be benign familial tremors. This was not a fatal disease, but it was an annoyance. Samuel's voice shook, his hands shook, and his head shook. As he got older, the tremors worsened. It was even hard for him to hold a pen. As governor, he dictated state papers for others to write. Sometimes his granddaughter, Elizabeth, who was 10 years old when he became governor, wrote his letters as he dictated.

He talked with Harvard graduates as well as with dock workers and criminals. The people listened to Samuel's ideas.

Samuel made a close friend in James Otis, a brilliant lawyer. Otis disliked Hutchinson, who was now lieutenant governor, as much as Samuel disliked him. Hutchinson was a rich man who thought wealthy men should rule the colony.

Otis was a great speaker. He was elected to the Massachusetts House of Representatives. Samuel helped him write his speeches and also edited the letters Otis wrote to the newspapers.

John Adams was another close friend of Samuel. The two were cousins, but they were very different. John Adams was a lawyer, and no one in Boston knew the law better than he did. He was not as rebellious as Samuel, but they both believed in the rights of man to make his own laws.

Samuel made friends with anyone who could help his cause of protecting the rights of the people. One unlikely friend was John Hancock.

Businessmen John Hancock listened to Samuel's opinions about British control of the colonies. Hancock's shipping business was affected by Britain's trade laws.

His family business was shipping. Because the British had so many limitations on trade, the wealthy Hancocks resorted to smuggling. Since British laws were hurting the business, John Hancock listened to Samuel's ideas of how the

British were controlling the colony.

The job as tax collector still wasn't working out for Samuel. Since he had not collected many taxes, he owed all the unpaid back taxes to the town. In 1764, Hutchinson and a few others accused Samuel of stealing the tax money, but the townspeople knew the truth. If people were having hard times, Samuel didn't make them pay. Samuel told the town meeting that he would quit the job. But the people elected him to another term. Samuel was pleased that the people believed in him.

On December 6, 1764, he married Elizabeth Wells. Because she had the same name as his dead wife, he called her Betsy. Not long after their marriage, Betsy was given a slave named Surry.

Samuel hated slavery and told Betsy that a slave could not live in his house. He filled out the necessary papers, and Surry moved in as a free person. Samuel believed that liberty was for all people: rich and poor, black and white, old and young.

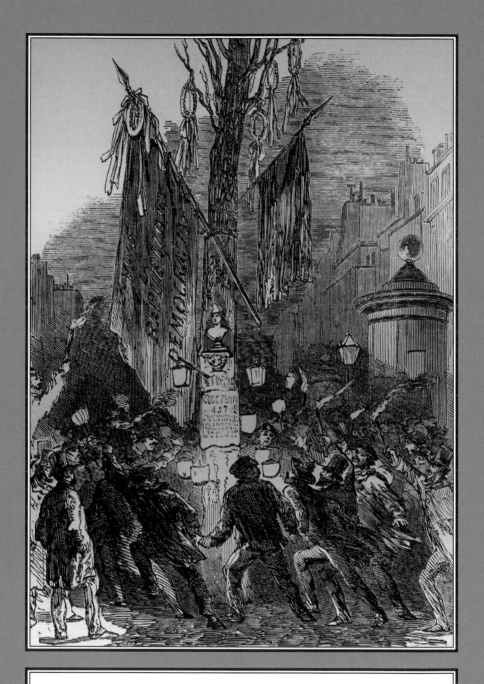

Samuel formed the Sons of Liberty, which would meet under an elm tree called the Liberty Tree. The members gathered to talk about colonists' rights.

3

Fighting Against Unfair Taxes

When the British Parliament passed the Stamp Act in 1765, Samuel Adams had something he could rally people around. The Stamp Act would take effect on November 1. It would require a tax stamp on printed materials. Newspapers, marriage licenses, diplomas, court documents, even playing cards needed stamps. The tax money raised from these tax stamps would go to the British government. It needed the money to pay for the Seven Years' War, also called the French and Indian War, which had been fought in North America.

Samuel wrote many letters to the newspapers

to tell readers about the tax. He claimed that the Stamp Act was illegal because the people had no representative in England who had voted on it.

Samuel told colonists how bad this tax was. He walked to stores and talked to shopkeepers and their customers. In taverns he spoke to bartenders and their customers. At the harbor, Samuel shared his ideas with dock workers.

The Sons of Liberty was formed with 300 workers from the harbor. Samuel knew they needed symbols of their group. He named a huge elm tree the Liberty Tree. The area under its branches was called Liberty Hall. Here the members gathered to talk about their rights.

Thomas Hutchinson's brother-in-law, Andrew Oliver, was appointed tax stamp distributor in

Samuel Adams walked nearly everywhere he went, even when he was governor. Some wealthy men felt he should travel in style. They presented him with a carriage and a team of horses. Samuel didn't believe public officials should take gifts, but he didn't want to insult these men. He used the carriage and horses during his terms as governor, but considered them a loan. When he retired from public office, he returned the horses and carriage.

the colony. Samuel told people this showed how one wealthy family was trying to control them.

One night, the Sons of Liberty made two dummies. One looked like Andrew Oliver. The other was a horned devil sticking out of a boot. It represented a leading British supporter of the Stamp Act. They hung the dummies from the Liberty Tree.

The next day a huge crowd surrounded the tree and talked about the dummies. British officials ordered the sheriff to cut down the dummies. But because there was such a large crowd, he was afraid, so he disobeyed.

That night, someone cut down the dummies. The Sons of Liberty carried them through the streets. A parade of townspeople marched to the wharf where Oliver had built a tax stamp office. They tore down the building and carried the wood to the street in front of Oliver's mansion. Here they built a bonfire and burned the dummies.

Some men threw rocks through the windows of Oliver's house. Others broke down the door with axes. Oliver and his family were upstairs. When Oliver stepped out on the balcony and asked what the mob wanted, they called for him to resign as stamp distributor. He promised he would, so the mob left.

Samuel was not a member of the mob, but many said he watched the flames of the bonfire from his nearby rooftop.

Several days later a mob rioted again. This time they attacked the houses of a judge, a customs official, and Hutchinson. The Hutchinson family fled before the mob reached their home. The mob tore down the walls and the roof and made a bonfire with books from the library. They stole silverware and money and threw paintings into the street.

This time the mob had gone too far. These were not Sons of Liberty, but thugs from gangs. Samuel needed to get them under control. He could manage men, because he was close to the people. Although he was an educated man, he was a poor man, like them.

The colonists in Boston rioted to protest the Stamp Act of 1765. Samuel spoke out against the law, which would provide more money from taxes to the British government.

Samuel talked to the leaders of the gangs and appealed to their patriotism. He planned a banquet for them, which was paid for by John Hancock. The leaders promised not to riot again.

When a member of the Massachusetts House of Representatives died, Samuel ran for the position and won a close race. He became the leader of those who were against the Stamp Act. His speeches in the House gave reasons the Stamp Act was unjust.

Samuel decided to write letters to other colonies. The Stamp Act would not affect just Boston. On November 1, it would be the law in all the British colonies. Samuel told leaders in other colonies what was going on in Boston.

Samuel also helped his friend James Otis organize the Stamp Act Congress. Leaders from nine of the thirteen colonies met in New York City to talk about the Stamp Act.

On November 1, the church bells in Boston rang slowly. Flags were flown at half-mast. More dummies were hung from the Liberty Tree. Courts were closed so that no stamps were needed on paper documents. Ships were not unloaded in the harbor. In other colonies, the same type of actions occurred.

Lawmakers in Britain were dismayed by the colonists' reactions. They didn't want to back down, but in early 1766 they voted to repeal the Stamp Act.

When news reached Boston, the city celebrated. Colorful streamers hung in the Liberty Tree. Church bells rang, musicians paraded through the streets, and fireworks exploded overhead. John Hancock had a dinner for his friends, and placed casks of wine on the commons for the townspeople.

But Samuel was not pleased with the repeal of his Stamp Act. Although he didn't say it, he wanted the colonies to rule themselves. But the time was not right for independence. He had to convince more people to dislike British rule.

The British Parliament passed the Declaratory Act. It said that Parliament could make laws for the colonies, which included taxing them. Samuel hoped the lawmakers would pass a new tax. He wanted the colonists angry enough that they would break away from Britain.

Samuel set out to convince more people to his way of thinking. Although he had known Hancock for several years, he now took him to political meetings. Hancock was one of the wealthiest men in the colonies. Before the election of 1766, Samuel talked to friends about who should run for the House of Representatives. Samuel suggested John Hancock, and he was elected.

In 1767, Britain passed the Townshend Acts. These were trade taxes on paint, tea, lead, paper, and glass brought into the colonies. Britain also began enforcing the Navigation Acts, which said the colonists could bring in goods only from British nations. Now Samuel had another issue to rile the people of Boston against the British.

Samuel organized the Sons of Liberty to hang dummies of British officials from the Liberty Tree. He called on townspeople to buy no British goods. He helped write a circular letter to other colonies' legislatures telling them that the new taxes were wrong.

The Sons of Liberty took mob actions. If a shopkeeper sold British goods, they threw rocks through the store windows. They also put signs on the stores, telling others that the stores carried British products.

John Hancock's shipping business brought in many goods from non-British nations. Before this time, customs officials had not inspected his ships for smuggled goods. But now the Navigation Acts were being enforced. When Hancock's new ship, the *Liberty*, docked with a load of smuggled wine, a customs official boarded it. The crew pushed him into a room and nailed it shut while they unloaded the wine.

Anchored in Boston Harbor was a British warship. Two customs officials climbed on the *Liberty* and claimed it had broken the law. British sailors towed the *Liberty* to the warship and tied the ships together so the Sons of Liberty couldn't rescue it.

Hancock never got his ship back. But the Sons of Liberty showed loyalty to Hancock. They threw bricks at the houses of the customs

In accordance with the Navigation Acts, British customs officers were permitted to inspect American ships for smuggled goods.

officials and broke the windows. Some men stole one official's small boat and burned it.

British officials thought that Samuel was behind all the mischief. They called him the most dangerous man in the colony. Hutchinson said Samuel was the one who controlled the people and caused them to riot.

With the people so stirred up, officials in Britain decided to send soldiers to restore order. This gave Samuel one more issue to fight–the presence of British soldiers.

In September 1768, Samuel held a meeting to gain support for his plan to stop the British king from sending troops to Boston. But he was too late. Soon the harbor would be filled with ships bearing soldiers.

Political Genius

Samuel Adams devoted all his time to the cause of liberty. If he wasn't thinking about it, he was writing about it. If he wasn't writing about it, he was talking about it.

This left no time for regular work. He earned a little bit for being clerk of the House of Representatives. But his brewery went out of business. Rumors were that John Hancock supported him, and other friends gave food to his family.

The expected arrival of British soldiers was of great interest to Samuel. In early fall at a town meeting, leaders talked about giving the town's guns and

Faneuil Hall was built between 1740 and 1742. It was used for town meetings in Boston.

ammunition to the people. The townspeople voted against the idea, and the guns stayed in the meeting hall.

It was Samuel's plan to let everyone know about the soldiers. He planned a meeting of representatives from all the towns in the colony. About a hundred men attended the meeting in

September 1768. The British governor told the men to go home, but they did not.

Instead, they talked about the problem. But farmers from western Massachusetts were not very upset about the British soldiers coming to Boston. It didn't affect people living in the country. The representatives decided to send a petition to the king, asking him not to send soldiers.

But they were too late. British warships were seen off the coast. The meeting broke up before ships carrying soldiers anchored and pointed their cannons at Boston.

The next day, hundreds of soldiers carrying guns and ammunition came ashore. They wore bright red coats and black three-cornered hats. Soldiers marched through town to the beat of drums and the playing of fifes.

Some soldiers pitched tents on Boston Common. Others were led to the town meeting hall. Before they laid out their gear, they took the guns and ammunition the townspeople had left there.

Samuel could not keep the soldiers out, but he could make their lives miserable. He started his own news service and printed lies about the redcoats, writing that the soldiers beat up boys and terrorized women. His stories noted that the soldiers fired guns on the Sabbath.

Even though Samuel knew these stories weren't true, he needed to rile the citizens. His articles were reprinted in newspapers in other colonies. Many people believed what Samuel wrote about the redcoats was true.

Some of the soldiers were rude to the townspeople. They pushed them around when they met them on the street. But the townspeople were also rude to the soldiers and called them bad names.

Samuel encouraged

Samuel Adams wrote countless letters to newspapers. He wanted to sway readers to his point of view about liberty. He would write one letter and sign his name. Then he would write another letter which said he agreed with the letter written by Samuel Adams. He would sign a different name to the second letter. That made it seem like more people thought like he did. He wrote under at least 100 different names.

British ships are seen here entering Boston harbor. King George III sent British soldiers to Boston to stop the protests by the colonists.

boys to throw snowballs at the soldiers. Sometimes the boys threw rotten eggs. Even Samuel's dog Queue was mean to the soldiers. He bit them whenever he could. The soldiers shot at the dog and wounded him several times, but he always recovered.

For some time Samuel had been writing letters to members of the British Parliament. He wanted them to fire the British governor. Blamed for all the unrest in Boston, the governor was recalled to Britain in 1769. When he sailed away, the townspeople celebrated with bonfires and ringing bells. But that left Samuel's enemy, Thomas Hutchinson, as acting governor.

The Sons of Liberty forbid people from buying British goods. Some boys painted a sign making fun of shopkeepers who bought from the British. They were putting it in front of one shop when a man named Ebenezer Richardson tried to stop them. The boys threw rocks at him.

Richardson ran home and got a gun. From his window he shot at the boys with swanshot, much like BB's. Eleven-year-old Christopher Snyder was hit in the chest and died that night. Richardson was sent to jail but was later pardoned by the king.

Samuel Adams arranged a magnificent funeral for the boy. The funeral procession was led by 500 schoolchildren, marching two by two. Then six young men carried the small coffin. It was followed by 2,000 people from Boston. The boy was turned into a hero for the cause of liberty.

A few days later on Friday, some rope workers and soldiers got into a fight. It grew from pushing and shoving to hitting with clubs. Another incident followed on Saturday. By Monday morning, March 5, 1770, posters had been tacked near the waterfront. They stated that the soldiers were going to defend themselves.

No one knew who put up the posters, but many suspected it was not the soldiers. Instead it was done by someone who wanted to rouse the people of Boston. Some said Samuel had sent letters to nearby towns telling them that the help of liberty-loving citizens might be needed on March 5.

The town's mood was angry on that evening. A foot of snow covered the ground. Townspeople should have been by their fireplaces at home, but by seven o'clock bands of men were prowling the streets. A crowd had gathered at the foot of the Liberty Tree.

Someone climbed a church bell tower and rang the bell. Normally that was a signal that there was a fire. Soon church bells rang all over Boston. People poured onto the streets with water buckets. Many asked about the fire. But there was no fire. The bells were to call out a mob.

Bands of boys confronted soldiers. One soldier on King Street reacted to taunts and knocked a boy down. The boy yelled for help, which came immediately.

A crowd gathered and threw snowballs at the soldiers and at the guard post on King Street. The crowd knew that the soldier could not fire on them because this was a peace-keeping force and not a force at war. To open fire would take an order of a British official, not a military official.

The soldier got word to Captain Thomas Preston that he needed help. Preston led seven soldiers to King Street. The men loaded their guns, but Captain Preston told people

In March 5, 1770, tensions peaked and British soldiers fought with colonists at the Boston Customs House. Five Patriots died in what was called the Boston Massacre. Samuel wrote articles about the massacre and the news spread through the colonies.

that there would be no gunfire.

A townsman attacked a soldier with a stick and knocked him down. The soldier shot his gun when he heard the word "fire."

Captain Preston did not give the order. In

the total confusion, several people had yelled, "Fire?" as a question, wondering if there was a fire because of the church bells. Others in the mob yelled, "Fire!" or "Why don't you fire?" at the soldiers.

Random shots rang out. The crowd fell back, but not before men were shot. Three men died instantly. One man died within hours, and a fifth man died a few days later.

Officials managed to break up the crowd by sending Preston and his small group of soldiers to jail. They sent other soldiers, who had rushed to the scene, back to their quarters. The mob carried the dead and wounded away.

The next morning, Samuel spoke to a huge crowd at the town meeting hall. They voted to ask the governor to move the soldiers out of Boston to Castle William, an island in Boston Harbor.

Samuel and a committee presented the demands to the governor and his council. After some discussion, Hutchinson agreed to remove the regiment of soldiers that was involved in the gunfire. Samuel demanded all the soldiers leave town. Hutchinson said he needed time to think, but would give his answer by afternoon.

By the time Samuel returned to the town meeting, the crowd had grown and could no longer fit in the meeting hall. Three thousand people paraded past the place where the governor and his council met. They went to a bigger meeting hall, with the spillover crowd in the street.

Samuel, John Hancock, and others returned to the governor to hear his final answer. Hutchinson gave in and all the soldiers were removed from town.

On December 16, 1773, colonists dressed as American Indians boarded ships in Boston Harbor and threw chests of tea into the harbor. The colonists were protesting Britain's Tea Act.

Fanning the Flames of Revolution

amuel Adams arranged a huge funeral for the victims of the Boston Massacre, as he called the King Street fight. Thousands of people turned out for the long march to the cemetery.

Of course, in his articles for newspapers, he made it seem like the soldiers were totally at fault. He wanted the people in all the colonies to be against British rule. A committee headed by Samuel wrote the report the town meeting sent to Britain. It claimed that innocent people were fired on by the soldiers.

Samuel hoped for quick trials. When John

Adams was hired as one of the lawyers for the soldiers, Samuel was glad. His cousin John was the best lawyer in town. Boston would show the world that it believed in justice for all—even for British soldiers.

The trials were delayed for several months. John Adams wanted a fair trial. He made sure no Sons of Liberty were on the jury. Captain Preston's trial was first. Since he hadn't given the order to fire, he was found not guilty.

Next was the trial of the eight soldiers. Witnesses had seen two of the soldiers shoot two men. They were found guilty of manslaughter. It was unclear which of the remaining six soldiers had fired on the threatening mob. They were found not guilty.

Samuel was not pleased with the verdicts. He continued to tell his side of what happened that fateful night, although he wasn't there. And he promised that every year he would hold a memorial on March 5.

Parliament repealed all the Townshend Acts

except for the tax on tea. Samuel still wanted colonists not to buy things from the British. But times were hard, and people felt things would be better if trade started again between the colonies and Britain.

Colonists wanted to forget the hard feelings and live in peace with the British. Few people listened to Samuel anymore. Not many newspapers would print Samuel's articles about liberty. He called meetings to rally support against the British, but few people came. During this quiet period, Samuel never gave up. He said if necessary, he would stand alone against the British.

In November 1772, Samuel stood up in the Massachusetts House of Representatives and asked that a **Committee of Correspondence** be established. It was a committee of 21 men who wrote down the rights of the people and sent copies to other colonies. He wanted each colony to form its own committee. They could tell each other what the British were doing in their colonies.

The formation of these committees was a major step in uniting the colonies. It was not long before Britain gave the colonists something more to write about.

In the spring of 1773, Parliament passed the Tea Act. The tax on tea was the only one that had been kept of the Townshend Acts. But instead of paying it, the colonists had smuggled Dutch tea. Then Britain cut the price of tea from a British firm, but it kept the tax. Even with the tax, British tea would be much cheaper than the Dutch tea.

The British hoped the Americans would buy the cheap tea. It would prove that the price was more important than the taxation without representation the colonists always complained about.

Americans were angry. Did the British think the colonists could be fooled? Not with Samuel leading the fight! He wrote more letters, and he called more meetings under the Liberty Tree. People everywhere talked about the Tea Act.

The British had officers, or excisemen, in America to make sure the laws imposed by Britain were followed. An exciseman is shown here being tarred and feathered by colonists as a punishment.

Three ships loaded with tea arrived in Boston Harbor. The Sons of Liberty placed guards at the wharf. They would not let the tea be unloaded and demanded that the ships be sent back to Britain. Governor Hutchinson refused to send the ships back.

Samuel had a secret plan. He carefully organized a small group of men. Then on December 16, 1773, several thousand people, from Boston and the countryside, gathered for a meeting about the tea. They sent a messenger to ask the governor once more to send the ships back. As they awaited his answer, men gave fiery speeches. Toward dark, the messenger returned with the news that the governor wouldn't send the ships back.

"This meeting can do nothing more to save the country," Samuel stood up and shouted.

At this signal, men dressed as American Indians marched down the dark street to the wharf. Many people followed them to the harbor and watched as they climbed aboard the ships. They demanded that the sailors unlock the cargo holds. One by one the "Indians" carried tea chests to the deck and poured the tea into the water.

News spread to the other colonies about what was called the Boston Tea Party. Other colonies dumped tea from English ships into the water. But no tea party angered Parliament like the first one. Boston was seen as the leading city of revolt, and Samuel led Boston.

Britain demanded payment for the tea. Boston refused to pay, so Britain punished the people by closing Boston Harbor. British General Thomas Gage was appointed military governor. Five thousand British soldiers poured into Boston. Town meetings were forbidden.

Many people expected Samuel to be arrested and executed. But the colonists wouldn't say who had organized the revolt. The British could not prove that Samuel was involved.

> The "Indians" who dumped tea overboard at the Boston Tea Party were careful to make sure every tealeaf went into the water. The men even swept the deck to make sure all the tea was gone. But later when a couple of "Indians" were taking off their boots, they discovered that tealeaves had fallen inside. Both men saved the tea as historic relics. One bottle of tealeaves is on display at the Old State House and another in the Old North Church in Boston.

Samuel's long-time enemy, Thomas Hutchinson, sailed for Britain and never returned. Finally, Samuel had won the feud with the governor. Samuel wrote to other Committees of Correspondence. With the port closed, supplies could not be brought in. Other colonies sent food and money to help the people of Boston.

Colonial leaders decided it was time for all the colonies to meet. The Massachusetts House of Representatives elected Samuel to be a delegate to this meeting of the Continental Congress in Philadelphia.

The people of Boston didn't want Samuel to look like a poor man at the convention. His friends outfitted him in new shoes, clothes, and hat. Although he still shook with the tremors, he looked like a new man. He even had a new red cloak.

The Continental Congress opened in Carpenter's Hall on September 5, 1774. Fifty-six men represented 12 colonies. Georgia sent no delegates.

The convention delegates were from many different religions. They disagreed on who should open the meeting with prayer. Samuel wanted the delegates to compromise. Samuel, a strict Puritan, suggested that an Episcopalian should give the prayer. He said he "was no bigot, and could hear a prayer from a gentleman of piety and virtue, who was at the same time a friend to his country." The others agreed.

The Continental Congress mostly met as a group, but they also met in small committee meetings in taverns and boarding houses. This was the type of meeting where Samuel was at his best. He could convince men to see his views.

Although most of the leaders did not want war with Britain, they wanted the rights of free men. They formed a Continental Association, which called for the colonists to stop trade with Britain. Maybe this would make Britain repeal the laws against Boston. Before the delegates left, they pledged to help Massachusetts if it were attacked. Militias were to drill in all the colonies in case they were needed to fight. They set a date to meet again a few months later.

Samuel went back to Boston. The city under military rule, which meant there were no courts, no taxes collected to run the town, and no House of Representatives.

A Provincial Congress, an illegal meeting of representatives, had met in Massachusetts while Samuel was in Philadelphia. John Hancock was president and headed the Committee of Public Safety. His job was to raise and call out the **militia**. These men were called minutemen, because they could be ready to fight in one minute.

Through the winter, Samuel wrote to his friends in other colonies. He wanted to make sure they would support a war. Samuel thought this winter would be the last peaceful winter for some time. The time for independence was coming soon.

By spring, General Gage was ready to take control and arrest rebel leaders. Friends urged Samuel and Hancock to leave Boston.

The two leaders went to a meeting of the Provincial Congress in Concord. When the

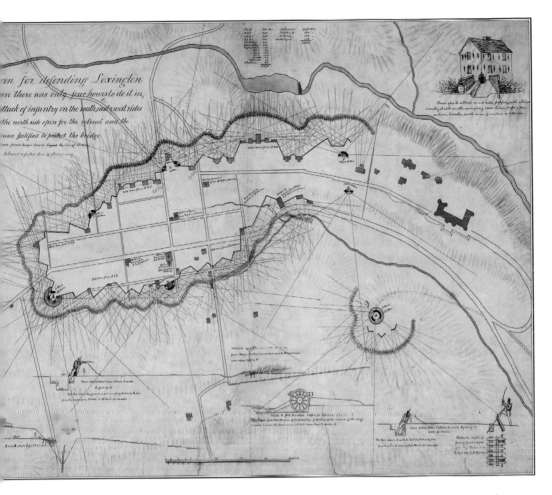

This map details the plan for defending Lexington from an infantry attack on the west, east, and south sides. The north side was left open for the Patriots to retreat.

meeting was over, they went to Lexington and stayed with friends. Messengers came to the house to tell them about odd movements of the troops in Boston.

Paul Revere rode to Lexington to tell Samuel and John Hancock that British troops were coming to arrest them.

A few days later, around midnight, Paul Revere rode to the house. He told the two leaders that British troops were crossing the Charles River. They were coming to arrest Samuel and

Hancock. Then they would march to Concord and take the guns and ammunition the colonists had stored there.

Half an hour later, William Dawes, another messenger sent from Boston, arrived with the same news. Hancock wanted to stay and fight. But Samuel argued that they were leaders, not soldiers. It was near daylight when they climbed in a buggy and took off across fields to avoid any British soldiers on the road.

Minutemen had assembled on the Lexington village green on that Wednesday morning, April 19, 1775. British soldiers marched toward them. The militia was warned not to fire unless fired upon.

It is not clear who actually fired first, a British soldier or a minuteman. But the shot was fired. And it was heard by Samuel and Hancock as they rumbled away in the carriage.

Samuel knew it was the first shot of the Revolutionary War. All that he had worked for was finally coming true. He smiled and said, "O! what a glorious morning is this!"

The Battle of Lexington on April 19, 1775, marked the start of the American Revolution. British soldiers killed eight colonial minutemen on the village green in Lexington, Massachusetts.

Father of American Independence

Samuel Adams and John Hancock traveled several miles to another house. There they learned of the American defeat at Lexington. After the smoke had cleared, eight Americans were dead and ten were wounded. Only one British soldier was wounded.

The defeat was not upsetting to Samuel. The war had started, and that was what was important. He hoped for a better report from the fight at Concord. And he got it.

At first the colonists in Concord watched as the soldiers took their small stash of weapons. But they were angered when the British set their Liberty Pole on fire. The militia attacked the redcoats guarding the North Bridge that led into town.

The soldiers retreated, and the militia followed. They shot at the redcoats from behind barns, trees, and stone walls. The British fell back near the house where Samuel and Hancock were staying. The two colonial leaders hid in a swamp nearby until the enemy was gone. Then they moved to another house. Later that evening, Samuel learned that the patriots had chased the redcoats almost to Boston.

Samuel hoped the Second Continental Congress, which met in May 1775, would declare independence from Britain. It did not. Instead, the delegates sent the Olive Branch Petition to King George III in Britain. It asked that peace be restored between the colonies and Britain.

Samuel and John Adams worked together to convince delegates at the Continental Congress to elect their candidates. They wanted John Hancock elected as president of Congress. This was done.

Samuel and John Adams wanted George Washington to command the Continental Army. Washington is shown in Cambridge, Massachusetts, on July 3, 1775.

Once Congress created the Continental Army, it needed a commander in chief. The Adams men wanted George Washington. They convinced other delegates that he was the man for the job.

Before Washington could take command, the British and Americans clashed at the Battle of Bunker Hill outside of Boston. The British claimed victory, because they had forced the Americans to retreat. But over 1,000 redcoats were killed or wounded, compared to about 400 Americans. On this basis, Samuel considered it an American victory.

He was also happy to learn that the king turned down the Olive Branch Petition. The king declared that the colonies were in a state of rebellion and the traitors should be punished.

In America only a third of the people wanted a war for independence. Another third opposed it, but a third was undecided. Even though his handwriting was shaky, Samuel wrote letters and articles for newspapers to influence people. He wanted independence now and believed that the time was finally right.

In June 1776 a motion was made in Congress that the colonies be made independent states. The vote was put off until July. Meanwhile, Thomas Jefferson of Virginia worked on the document that would declare independence.

Samuel talked to delegates one at a time. He listened to them, and then he shared his views, convincing one after another to vote his way.

Thomas Jefferson wrote the Declaration of Independence at the request of the Second Continental Congress. The document was approved on July 4, 1776.

On July 2, the delegates voted for independence. Two days later, on July 4, they approved the Declaration of Independence. When the official copy was ready, Hancock signed first, as he was president of the Congress. Samuel signed ninth.

Copies of the Declaration were read across the new nation. In Boston the reading was greeted with ringing bells, booming cannons, and cheering voices.

The war between the British and the Americans was hard fought. Many people felt that Britain would win and take over the colonies again. Samuel never lost faith that America would win. He believed strongly in the rights of man. The quest for liberty was worth fighting for, and he knew America should be a free country.

American soldiers suffered from cold, hunger, and exhaustion. Samuel didn't like it that wealthy John Hancock was living like a king when soldiers were starving. He talked to others congressmen about it. That made Hancock very angry, because he had given lots of money to the revolution. Hancock started an untrue rumor that Samuel didn't support Washington as head of the army. These harsh words caused a break between the two men.

In 1780, Hancock was elected governor of

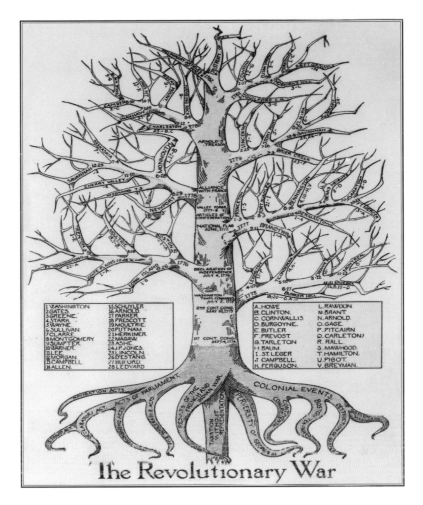

An artist's depiction of the Revolutionary War as a tree; issues like taxation without representation were the roots of rebellion that produced battles.

Massachusetts. Since the feud continued, Samuel was out of favor. His friends nominated him for secretary of state, but he lost the election. It did not bother him much. He felt a republic should elect anyone it wanted.

Still, he worked for the new nation. At one low point during the war, Samuel spoke to members of the Continental Congress about their attitudes. "If we wear long faces, long faces will become fashionable. The eyes of the people are upon us. The tone of their feelings is regulated by ours."

Samuel served in Congress until April 1781, six years after the Battle of Lexington. Then he went home to Boston, where he was elected to the state senate and soon became its president.

When the Americans won the war, Samuel knew triumph, and yet he was concerned about the new country. The loose federation between the states was not working well. The Constitution of the United States had been written, but it needed approval by the states.

In 1788, Samuel and Hancock were sent to the Massachusetts Constitutional Convention. The men had started talking to each other again,

Samuel, along with John Hancock and other members
of the Massachusetts Constitutional Convention, voted
to accept the Constitution of the United States.

and they both thought the Constitution would
make the federal government too strong.
Samuel believed the nation needed a bill of
rights that would protect freedom of speech and
freedom of religion.

While at the convention, Samuel learned
that his son was gravely ill. He rushed home
to be with his son. Samuel's son died, and
Samuel was devastated.

Samuel returned to the convention with a new attitude. He learned that the working-class people wanted the Constitution, and he was always faithful to the working class. Massachusetts voted to accept the Constitution. After the Constitution was the law of the land, a Bill of Rights was added, similar to what Samuel had suggested.

The next year, Samuel and Hancock renewed their friendship and forgave each other for earlier harsh words. Hancock ran for governor and Samuel ran for lieutenant governor. Both were elected year after year. In 1793, when Hancock died, Samuel became governor of Massachusetts.

Samuel's health was not good. His tremors had grown worse. But he gained new spirit when he was governor. He was very popular. He even received votes in 1796 for president of the United States, an office he did not seek. After Samuel was elected governor three times, he said he would not run again. At 74, he remains the oldest governor Massachusetts has ever had.

In his last years, Samuel's eyesight failed, and others read the newspaper to him. He always wanted to know what was happening in the new nation.

Samuel died on October 2, 1803. On the day of his funeral, shops in Boston closed, flags were flown at half-mast, and church bells tolled. In Washington, D.C., the new capital, congressmen wore black arm bands in honor of the Revolutionary War leader.

On July 4, 1795, Governor Samuel Adams and his friend Paul Revere laid the cornerstone on the New State House in Boston. The site of the building had been owned by John Hancock. Revere was hired to top the wooden dome with rolled copper. Later the dome was gilded with gold, and the structure was enlarged by several additions. Over two centuries later, the New State House is still the capitol building of Massachusetts.

Samuel Adams dreamed of a country where people could live with liberty. He spent his life making that vision come true. The United States of America was free to make its own laws.

GLOSSARY

British Parliament–the legislature of Great Britain.

colony–an area controlled by a distant nation.

Committee of Correspondence–a group of men who wrote to people in other colonies.

commons–land set aside for public use.

constitution–a set of principles.

Continental Congress–a group of men elected from all the colonies to decide policies.

customs official–a man who made sure imported goods were legal.

dame school–a school that was taught by a woman in her own home.

debt–something owed by one person to another.

delegate–a person who represents others.

federation–a loose organization of states.

Massachusetts General Court–the lawmaking government made up of two houses, the Council and the House of Representatives.

militia–a group of civilian men called into the military only during emergencies.

petition–a formal request.

repeal–to withdraw.

taxation without representation–taxes that were not voted on by the people or by their elected officials.

tyrant–a highly controlling ruler.

CHRONOLOGY

1722	Samuel Adams is born on September 27 to Deacon Samuel and Mary Adams in Boston.
1743	Earns master's degree from Harvard.
1749	Marries Elizabeth Checkley.
1757	IIis wife, Elizabeth, dies, leaving two small children.
1764	Marries Elizabeth Wells.
1765	Forms the Sons of Liberty; elected to the Massachusetts House of Representatives.
1770	Forces Governor Hutchinson to remove all troops from Boston.
1772	Forms the Committee of Correspondence.
1773	Plans the Boston Tea Party.
1774	Attends First Continental Congress.
1775	Escapes arrest before Battle of Lexington; attends Second Continental Congress.
1776	Signs Declaration of Independence.
1789	Elected lieutenant governor of Massachusetts.
1793	Becomes governor when John Hancock dies.
1794	Elected governor of Massachusetts in his own right.
1797	Retires to private life.
1803	Dies on October 2 at age 81, in Boston.

REVOLUTIONARY WAR TIME LINE ═══

1765	The Stamp Act is passed by the British. Violent protests against it break out in the colonies.
1766	Britain ends the Stamp Act.
1767	Britain passes a law that taxes glass, painter's lead, paper, and tea in the colonies.
1770	Five colonists are killed by British soldiers in the Boston Massacre.
1773	People are angry about the taxes on tea. They throw boxes of tea from ships in Boston harbor into the water. It ruins the tea. The event is called the Boston Tea Party.
1774	The British pass laws to punish Boston for the Boston Tea Party. They close Boston harbor. Leaders in the colonies meet to plan a response to these actions.
1775	The battles of Lexington and Concord begin the American Revolution.
1776	The Declaration of Independence is signed. France and Spain give money to help the Americans fight Britain. Nathan Hale is captured by the British. He is charged with being a spy and is executed.
1777	Leaders choose a flag for America. The American troops win some important battles over the British. General Washington and his troops spend a very cold, hungry winter in Valley Forge.
1778	France sends ships to help the Americans win the war. The British are forced to leave Philadelphia.

1779	French ships head back to France. The French support the Americans in other ways.
1780	Americans discover that Benedict Arnold is a traitor. He escapes to the British. Major battles take place in North and South Carolina.
1781	The British surrender at Yorktown.
1783	A peace treaty is signed in France. British troops leave New York.
1787	The U.S. Constitution is written. Delaware becomes the first state in the Union.
1789	George Washington becomes the first president. John Adams is vice president.

FURTHER READING ══════════════

Farley, Karin Clafford. *Samuel Adams: Grandfather of His Country.* Austin, TX: Raintree/Steck~Vaughn Publishers, 1995.

Fradin, Dennis Brindell. *Samuel Adams: The Father of American Independence.* New York: Clarion Books, 1998.

Fritz, Jean. *Why Don't You Get a Horse, Sam Adams?* NY: Coward, McCann & Geoghegan, Inc., 1974.

Kent, Deborah. *Lexington and Concord.* Danbury, CT: Children's Press, 1997.

Kroll, Steven. *The Boston Tea Party.* NY: Holiday House, 1998.

Moore, Kay. *If You Lived at the Time of the American Revolution.* NY: Scholastic, 1998

Penner, Lucille Recht. *The Liberty Tree: The Beginning of the American Revolution.* NY: Random House, 1998.

Weber, Michael. *The American Revolution.* Austin, TX: Raintree/ Steck~Vaughn Publishers, 2000.

PICTURE CREDITS ══════════════

INDEX

ABOUT THE AUTHOR ════════

Award-winning author **VEDA BOYD JONES** is the author of 27 books, including children's historical novels, children's biographies and nonfiction books, a picture book, romance novels, and a coloring book. Other published works include over 150 articles and stories in children's and other magazines and articles in reference books. Jones earned an MA in history at the University of Arkansas and currently teaches for the Institute of Children's Literature. She and her husband, Jimmie, have three sons, Landon, Morgan, and Marshall.

Senior Consulting Editor **ARTHUR M. SCHLESINGER, JR.** is the leading American historian of our time. He won the Pulitzer Prize for his book *The Age of Jackson* (1945), and again for *A Thousand Days* (1965). This chronicle of the Kennedy Administration also won a National Book Award. He has written many other books, including a multi-volume series, *The Age of Roosevelt*. Professor Schlesinger is the Albert Schweitzer Professor of the Humanities at the City University of New York, and has been involved in several other Chelsea House projects, including the Colonial Leaders series of biographies on the most prominent figures of early American history.